Live Like a **Vulcan,**

Love Like a **Wookiee,**

Laugh Like a **Hobbit**

Live Like a Vulcan, Love Like a Wookiee, Laugh Like a Hobbit

LIFE LESSONS *from* POP CULTURE

Robb Pearlman

Smart Pop Books
An Imprint of BenBella Books, Inc.
Dallas, TX

Live Like a Vulcan, Love Like a Wookiee, Laugh Like a Hobbit © 2021 by BenBella Books

Cover Illustrations © 2021 by Jason Kayser

BenBella Books, Inc.
10440 N. Central Expressway
Suite 800
Dallas, TX 75231
smartpopbooks.com
benbellabooks.com
Send feedback to feedback@benbellabooks.com

BenBella and *Smart Pop* are federally registered trademarks.

Printed in the United States of America
10 9 8 7 6 5 4 3 2 1

Library of Congress Control Number: 2021020408
ISBN 9781953295828
eISBN 9781637740118

Editing by Rachel Phares
Copyediting by Michael Fedison
Proofreading by Jenny Bridges and Sarah Vostok
Text design and composition by Aaron Edmiston
Cover design and illustration by Jason Kayser
Printed by Lake Book Manufacturing

Special discounts for bulk sales are available.
Please contact bulkorders@benbellabooks.com.

For Linda Kaplan and David Harmon

Main Menu

Main Menu

(continued)

"An unexpected pleasure."

—The Wizard of Oz

I pushed against the tavern's massive oak door, but it would not yield. I shook off the disappointment and pushed again. Harder. Stiffening my arms, leaning over, and pressing both hands firmly against the door's splintering, worn facade. Nothing.

I was as frustrated as I was exhausted. It had been a long day, and as much as I wanted to sleep, I knew I wouldn't rest—couldn't rest—until I was able to rid myself of the hunger that had walked with me these last few hours. The dim, gaslit corridor was just bright enough for me to find a placard written in English, Spanish, and grammatically incorrect Elvish, indicating that the pub would be open all night to accommodate weary travelers.

I looked around the doorway for a latch or lock that would reveal the source of the blockade. Finding none, I peered through the square of glass at the top of the door and saw no one but an Elder, his head bowed in quiet contemplation, sitting at a small table, which, like nearly every table in the room, was piled high with glasses, plates, and soiled napkins. I spotted a bar beyond the Elder and the tables where I could quickly eat before making my way to my room for a much-needed rest.

I took a step back, a deep breath, and threw my shoulder into the door. Again, I failed to move the door an inch, but the thudding sound was loud enough to garner the Elder's attention. I watched him look up. I held my breath, steeling myself for whatever the consequences would be for disturbing the old man's meditation.

"PULL!" he shouted.

I stepped back again and followed his instructions. The door swung toward me and brought the faint sounds of John Williams's *Superman* score and the overpowering aroma of fried foods with it. I stepped over the threshold. The physical exertion of trying to open the door, the heavy load I'd been carrying all day, my hunger, and the surprisingly harsh overhead fluorescent lighting all conspired to make me feel even more off-balance and awkward than I usually did. How would I make my way through the labyrinth of chairs and tables, around the Elder, and to the bar without knocking into anything and everything?

As usual, I was traveling solo, with only a book for company. It was neither the kind of book I would particularly recommend to anyone, nor was it bad enough to warrant a one-star review, but it was small and lightweight, and sufficiently interesting to keep me occupied while I sat alone. In fact, I'd traveled with this particular book—a novelization of a film I'd seen as a child—for years. Its spine was broken enough for me to fold over and hold in one hand while I ate with the other, and its pages stained enough that the ketchup I would inevitably spill on it wouldn't warrant too much gnashing of teeth. Like an old friend who kept repeating the same stories, it was comfortingly familiar and pleasant, reliable company.

As expected, I bumped my way through the tavern's closely set tables and chairs. As I approached the Elder—still the one human impediment between me and the bar—I couldn't help but admire the degree to which he was able to regain his composure and restart his meditation after being disturbed by my door-banging. I didn't want to trouble him again, but my fear of offending people overrides my fear of engaging with them, so I was compelled to acknowledge his kindness.

"Thanks for your help with the door. I would have been out there all night," I said. I noticed that his head was bowed not in silent contemplation, but to better see the game of *Tetris* playing on the phone he held in his lap.

"I couldn't let you suffer out there," the Elder said without looking up. "But now that you're inside, prepare for a bit of a wait. The waiter's in the back, either crying or drinking. Probably both." I wasn't offended by the Elder's lack of eye contact—I could see that he was a microsecond away from maneuvering a long green rectangle between two blocks. "The poor fellow's been the only person working this whole place. I'm surprised he didn't lock the door hours ago." The Elder paused his game and finally looked at me. His eyes were bright blue and kinder than I'd imagined they would be. "You might as well take a seat here and wait for him." The old man pocketed his phone into a hidden fold of his flowing gray-and-white robes. He leaned over and pulled up a chair from a nearby table. He patted the seat, inviting me to join him.

"Oh, I don't want to interrupt," I said, pointing to the three empty seats already surrounding the table.

"It's no bother at all. My friends and I were just talking about . . . well, all manner of things. Big things and small things. There's always room for one more." The Elder seemed to sense my hesitancy. Had the tavern been crowded, I could have easily let myself get lost, alone, in the crowd; but emptiness offered no camouflage. I felt ripples of social anxiety lapping against my chest.

"I insist," he said. I mumbled thanks and sat in the chair. As I let my backpack slip off my shoulders and drop to the floor behind me, I flinched at the thought of having accidentally bent the autographed poster I'd bought earlier in the day. I inspected the poster tube and, finding it still in pristine condition, turned my attention toward a special menu posted on the wall. The tavern's offerings were limited to burgers, pizza, and nachos—the kinds of things a kitchen could get out quickly and in large enough quantities to accommodate the larger-than-normal crowds in town for the event.

I could feel the ripples of my anxiety growing into waves. I forced a smile on my face and braced myself for what I knew would be a terribly awkward meal. I would have to eat quickly if I wanted to escape the uncomfortable silences and retreat into the comfortable silence of my hotel room without embarrassing myself. But in the meantime, I vowed to keep that smile on my face for as long as I could.

"Ah, here they are now," said the Elder, directing his gaze across the room.

My feigned smile became genuine. For it was then that I saw, emerging from the gender-neutral, pan-species, and all-fandom restroom on the opposite side of the tavern, a Vulcan, a Wookiee, and a Hobbit.

"No choice, huh?"

—Blade Runner

" It's nice to meet you," I said sheepishly as the Vulcan, the Wookiee, and the Hobbit took their seats around the table. "Are you sure I'm not intruding?" I secretly hoped one of them would give me an easy out, but they all talked over one other, enthusiastically insisting that I remain seated at the table.

The Hobbit threw his legs over the side of his chair and held his empty pint glass aloft. "Did the waiter stop crying yet? I need a refill."

"Not yet," said the Elder. "I think he expected you to be gone longer." Judging by the way they were dressed, I would have agreed with the waiter. The quality of their costumes was truly remarkable. I imagined it would be especially difficult for the Wookiee to maneuver around a public restroom without getting layers of "con crud" matted in their fur. I tried to casually scan the entirety of the Wookiee's fur-lined body to find a seam or zipper showing just how it was put together, but there was simply too much to take in. The color of the Vulcan's pointy ears matched his skin tone perfectly, and his arched brows and haircut seemed as natural and on point as the crease in his uniform's pants and the shine on his boots. And though I saw, because he was still hanging them over the chair and directly facing me, that the Hobbit was wearing stick-on protective soles on the bottoms of his feet, they really did seem sturdy and hairy enough to make a journey across Middle-earth.

"Your cosplays all look so great," I said. "But I wouldn't have thought you'd all be together."

The Vulcan raised an eyebrow. The Hobbit smiled and raised his empty mug a bit higher in hopes the waiter would come back. The Wookiee cocked their head. The Elder stroked his beard thoughtfully and asked, "Why is that?"

"Well, it's sort of a blending of franchises here. The ultimate mash-up. I mean, I get it, I'm into it all, but it's a bit surprising to see all of you together."

"Add this to the list," the Hobbit said with a giggle.

"He means the list of things that pop culture has taught us," explained the Elder. "That's what we were talking about before you joined our little party."

"He's been doing most of the talking," the Hobbit stage-whispered in my direction, gesturing toward the Elder with a theatrical flourish. How much longer would he keep his arm up?

"Well, that's just because you've all been kind enough to let me prattle on," the Elder said.

"Each of our . . . species . . . was taught to respect our elders," said the Vulcan with a raise of his eyebrow.

"Pop culture taught you that?" I asked.

"Yes," the Vulcan replied.

"He's like Gandalf," the Hobbit grinned.

"Or Obi-Wan," offered the Wookiee.

"Or Spock," said the Vulcan, casually tossing a fry into his mouth.

"Spock?" I asked incredulously. "I'm not sure about that."

"In *Star Trek*, there's no direct analogue to the old, wizened man. No offense," the Vulcan added quickly, glancing toward the oldest among them. The Elder brushed off the slight. The Vulcan continued, "Guinan? Maybe. Mr. Atoz? Only seen once. Picard? Close, but he doesn't quite fit the bill of aiding the hero on his epic journey, as he's arguably the hero of *TNG*. The closest is Spock."

I considered this for a moment. "Spock grew old for sure—very old for a half human, in fact. And he became a diplomat, worked with Picard on Romulus, but he wasn't necessarily a mentor who advised the protagonist throughout his journey. Maybe Sarek . . . maybe. But Spock?"

The Vulcan raised a perfectly arched eyebrow again and said, "If you look at *The Animated Series*, which is canon by the way, Spock goes back in time to help his younger self. And then, in the 2009 movie, Spock Prime helps the Kelvin Timeline Spock. And if you want to get meta, it looks like Leonard Nimoy did the same for Zachary Quinto in real life when he took over the role of Spock, offering guidance and support. It is the perfect example of how pop culture can be applied to real life!"

"Ugh, don't get me started on the JJ-verse," I groaned. "All of those lens flares! It just wasn't my *Enterprise*."

"But it's someone's *Enterprise*," remarked the Wookiee. "Some people like the stuff they grew up with. Others like the things they were introduced to by someone they trust. Some people just like stuff because it speaks to them in a way that nothing else does. There's nothing wrong with letting people like what they like and love what they love."

"And whether or not I like something really has no bearing on what you think of it," the Vulcan interjected. "As much as we fans want to claim our favorite pop culture properties for ourselves, they're not our creations. Sure, we can write fanfic and play with action figures, and make up characters and stories in RPGs and MMORPGs, but we can't dictate the stories others tell us. Just think: if Gene Rodden-berry had listened to fans' outrage, *The Next Generation* never would have made it onto the air—and that became lots of people's introduc-tion to *Star Trek*. That was *their Star Trek*. And though lots of people have lots of issues with the Abrams-produced *Trek* trilogy, his *Star Wars* sequel trilogy, or even George Lucas's own *Star Wars* prequel trilogy—"

"I've got some issues," interrupted the Wookiee.

"And that's fine!" the Vulcan continued. "It's healthy to have opin-ions, to acknowledge imperfections, to let our imaginations run wild with 'what could have been,' or 'what if,' but we must also accept the fact that these were the stories the storytellers wanted to tell. No fan has the authority to tell storytellers what their own stories are, and they don't have the right to tell other fans what they should or shouldn't like."

"Or even who is and isn't a fan," remarked the Elder.

I thought for a moment. "But . . . but . . ." My thoughts became as cloudy as a nebula as I looked for a reason, some small justification, to prove that I was right, but the black-and-white views of pop culture I'd proudly espoused until now suddenly felt as outdated as a TV with a 4:3 aspect ratio. I came up empty. "You're right," I admitted. "I guess I never really thought about it all that much. I mean, I love *Star Wars* and *Star Trek* . . ."

"And *The Lord of the Rings*?" asked the Hobbit eagerly.

"Yep, that, too, but I can't say that I like every single thing in all of it," I replied.

"So you already appreciate how liking one thing doesn't mean you have to automatically dislike something else. And if something isn't for you, then that's okay, too. It may be for someone else. You can still appreciate it all. The only binaries that should matter are the suns above Tatooine and the stars at the start of the Federation-Klingon War. So few things in life have to be an 'either/or.' There's room for Marvel and DC on any shelf. Your screens can play both *Star Wars* and *Star Trek*. You can play *Mass Effect* as much as *Halo*."

"But what if it's something *nobody* likes?" I asked.

"Then you'll lose a fortune trying to resell its tie-in action figures on eBay," said the Elder.

"But if you keep them mint-in-box and wait fifteen years for it to become a camp classic, you'll *make* a fortune!" added the Wookiee.

"You're going to need a bigger boat."

—*Jaws*

The Hobbit was still holding his empty mug aloft when the Vulcan pointed to a ripped seam beneath his friend's arm. As the Hobbit slipped out of his green jacket, the Wookiee began searching in one of the pockets of their bandolier until they found a needle and thread. The Vulcan took the jacket, the needle, and the thread and promptly began sewing up the seam. I remarked at how easy and effortlessly systematic this impromptu triage was.

"We've seen *Jaws*," said the Vulcan through gritted teeth, concentrating on making the stitches as tiny as possible.

"*Jaws*?" I asked. "Did a great white bite into his jacket?"

They all smiled. Well, I assumed the Wookiee smiled; it was hard to tell. "Not quite, but we learned two important things from *Jaws*," said the Elder.

"And what are those?" I asked, curious about what this next piece of pop culture wisdom would be.

"First," said the Hobbit, finally giving up hope that the waiter would arrive and setting his mug on the table, "is that nobody knows everything about everything. Sheriff Brody knew he needed help out on the water, so he brought Quint and Hooper on the boat with him. And though they were an uneasy alliance at best, each of the men recognized that they all brought something important to the table that the others couldn't. For instance," the Hobbit continued pleasantly, "I know enough about myself to know that not only do I not know how to sew, I don't have the patience to learn."

"Or the perfectionism it takes to do it up to your own standards," the Elder interjected.

"Exactly," agreed the Hobbit. "And unlike my friend here, who walks around with more pockets than I can count," he said, gesturing toward the Wookiee, "my own pockets are usually too full of snacks and panel tickets and program guides to have room for a needle and thread."

"Pockets are so handy!" the Wookiee exclaimed, pointing to each one on the bandolier slung across their chest. "I have a needle and thread in this one, breath mints in this one, and cash in this one. Which reminds me," they said to the Hobbit. "You still owe me for breakfast."

"I know," replied the Hobbit.

"And second breakfast, too!" the Wookiee reminded him.

"I know, I know! My point is that, like Sheriff Brody, I know and accept my own limitations, and know when to ask for—and accept—help. Sometimes begrudgingly, but I accept it eventually! Then, in turn, I'm freer to *offer* help. For example, my friends here know I can get around and through crowds quicker and easier than they can."

"It's true," said the Vulcan, looking up from his stitchwork. "I don't know how he does it, but he manages to get everywhere five minutes before we even leave. It's like he beams himself places."

"I may be small, but I'm nimble," said the Hobbit. "So when it's time for us to get to a panel, I go on ahead and save our place in line. We each have skills or perspectives that complement each other's." He pointed to the Wookiee. "Like their ability to see over anyone's heads. And his knack for keeping us on schedule," he continued, pointing at the Vulcan. "We're stronger together as a Fellowship."

"That all makes sense," I said, "but what's the second thing you learned from *Jaws*?"

The Hobbit took a deep breath. "No matter how prepared you think you are, you're always going to need a bigger boat." He paused to look around once more for the waiter and, not finding him, continued. "Brody, Quint, and Hooper thought they had their shark-capturing mission under control: chum, calm waters, lots of buoys, each other. What more could they need? Well, as it turned out, a lot. A bigger boat, for one, but also even more buoys, bigger guns, and, in Quint's case"—the Hobbit gritted his teeth—"chain-mail underwear."

We all squirmed in our seats a little. The Hobbit composed himself and continued. "It's easy to be unprepared. It's possible to be prepared. It's impossible to be overprepared. We've been wearing cosplays at events for years and, until today, none of us suffered any rips or tears. Had we gone home without using the needle and thread, we could have thought it was a waste of time to have it in the first place, but, as fate would have it, we did need it. Well, *I* needed it, and I'm glad we prepared for it. I've yet to use the hand sanitizer my Wookiee friend has been carrying around, too, but I'm glad they have it in case I need it."

"You . . . you really should be using it," the Wookiee suggested, shivering.

"Nah, I'm good," said the Hobbit, showing us his clean-ish hands. "And I haven't had to dip into this flask I've hidden in my vest yet, but if the waiter doesn't show up soon, I'll be glad I have it!"

"Wait, you've been carrying around a flask but don't have room for a needle and thread?" asked the Wookiee. "For years?"

"That's neither there nor back again. It's here in case we need it. I've brought a bigger boat!" said the Hobbit, who suddenly broke out into the biggest and brightest smile I'd ever seen. The waiter had finally arrived.

"You meddling kids."

—Scooby-Doo! & Batman: The Brave and the Bold

The waiter looked like Pietro Maximoff. Not the *WandaVision* one, the *Age of Ultron* one. During the Battle of Sokovia. Right after he's shot. Stringy gray hair clung to his face, and he wore a soiled, sweat-stained, and slightly bloodied blue-and-white uniform. He approached us panting, as if he'd just finished running for hours.

"Sorry for the wait. Refills?" he asked between breaths, gasping like he'd just tried to single-handedly neutralize the Ultron Offensive. *Maybe this is really just a very good Quicksilver cosplay?* I thought.

"Please, another round of everything," said the Elder. "And our new friend here would like some food, too," he added, gesturing toward me.

As I ordered a pizza, a single tear Fassbendered its way down the waiter's cheek.

"Are . . . are you OK?" I asked.

"Sorry," he said, wiping the sweat, grime, and tear from his face. "It's just that I've been the only server here all day and I'm exhausted. I thought taking a break in the back would help, but . . ." He lost his words and leaned into the table as if his body was accepting defeat.

"There's no rush," I said, as the Hobbit gave me a stern look and pointed to his empty glass. "I mean, um, sorry?"

"No, no, *I'm* sorry," the waiter said, standing a bit straighter, wiping his eyes again, and dragging his hair behind his ears.

The Hobbit turned in his seat toward the waiter. "I don't understand why they'd only have one person on duty tonight," he said. "It's not like they didn't know the con was happening."

"We're usually well staffed," the waiter replied miserably. "Mostly the owner's family."

"You're saying Mr. Marriott himself waits tables?" asked the Wookiee skeptically.

"No, no. This place isn't run by the hotel; it's like, a lease or something. Anyway, a bunch of us regular, nonfamily employees put in for vacation time weeks ago so we could go to the convention and have some fun. But I got a call this morning from my boss—he said his entire family got sick and he begged me to come in. I figured I could give up a day of fun and it would be good money, but he didn't tell me I'd be the only one out here. I never would have agreed had I known it'd just be me and the cook. It's literally killing me."

"It's only metaphorically killing you, my dear boy," the Elder corrected. "Did he say what made every member of the family sick?" he asked suspiciously.

"He didn't, but it must have been pretty bad for them all to get it. I guess it was something they ate at home because I'm totally fine. I offered to stop by their house and bring them soup or whatever from here, but he told me I'd better stay away or I'd get sick, too. And he made a point to say that if I got sick or couldn't work today, they'd lose so much money they wouldn't be able to keep the lease here, so they'd have to close the restaurant, and we'd all wind up losing our jobs," said the waiter.

"Wow, that's really too bad," I replied. The waiter smiled ruefully and walked away.

"This situation calls for some meddling kids," said the Elder.

"How do you mean?" I asked.

"We've all watched enough television programs to see that many problems, whether they're big or small, are often blamed on extraneous, unexplainable, and uncontrollable forces, when they're actually man-made," the Elder posited to the group.

"Nobody calls them 'programs' anymore," said the Hobbit.

"Shows? Streams? Twitches? Whatever they are," said the Elder, leaning in conspiratorially, "whether it's *Scooby-Doo* or *E.T.* or *Stranger Things* or *Nancy Drew* or *The Walking Dead*, pop culture has shown us that the true Big Bads of most terrible situations are not monsters or ghosts or zombies or any number of innocent scapegoats, but old men using literal scare tactics to try to hold on to the positions of privilege and wealth they feel are slipping away. Whether they're trying to keep money or power for themselves, trying to cheat others out of what they're rightfully due, or are part of a giant corporate or government scheme that's attempting to either cover up what they're actively doing or cover up what they already did—and messed up—they'll stop at nothing to get what they want, or what they think they deserve. And though these men may see others as abstract impediments that must be eliminated or worked around, they ultimately see themselves as above the law, morality, or responsibility. It's like their status and privilege renders them constitutionally incapable of seeing anyone as a true threat. Especially if that threat is from someone they view as inferior or less powerful." The Elder stopped to take a breath.

The Wookiee cocked their head to the side. "So you're saying that basically everything that's wrong is the fault of old men?"

We all looked at the Elder. "Well, not everything," he conceded. "But let's face it, most of the faces hiding beneath the masks Freddie pulled off were old men. And Negan and other survivors are far worse than any zombie on *The Walking Dead*."

The waiter returned with our drinks and cleared away our empties. "So where are your other coworkers? Couldn't any of them come in to help?" asked the Vulcan.

The waiter wiped down the table. "The cook came in. He's been in the back since this morning. I don't know what happened with everyone else. I guess they all said no to working or couldn't come in? We're not all that friendly and I'm not one to ask questions. Maybe they got sick, too? I dunno. Anyway, I'll be right back with your food."

The Vulcan leaned in. "You're right. Think about it. Isn't it just a little odd that the one day the entire family gets sick is the one day they all have passes to do something fun together? And this poor guy is told two things to make him afraid: one, if he investigates too much, he'll get sick, too; and two, if he doesn't do as his boss asks, he's putting himself and everyone he works with in jeopardy of losing their livelihoods. And he's admitted to not only being separated from the rest of his crew, but also the kind of person who doesn't ask too many questions, so it's unlikely they'll team up to fight back against the boss or try to find out the truth. A bunch of kids on bikes could take down a company or Goonie their way into finding hidden treasure, but one kid on a bike is just one kid on a bike."

"Exactly," said the Elder. "Now I'm no teen detective—"

"That's for sure," agreed the Hobbit.

"—but it all seems rather suspicious," the Elder continued. "*Too* suspicious, if you ask me. Yes, it's totally possible that the entire family came down with an illness at the same time. And it's possible that the money lost on this one day in particular would doom the entire business. And it's possible that our waiter and the cook were the only two people available and well enough to work. And it's possible that the owner of a family business was desperate to keep his sole source of income afloat. All of these are possible. Probable? Who knows. But possible? Yes. But we could really learn something from Velma, Daphne, Fred, Shaggy, and Scooby-Doo, or all of those kids on bikes, from Elliott and Michael trying to save E.T. to Eleven, Mike, Dustin, Lucas, and the other kids from Hawkins: sometimes the only way to really get to the bottom of things, to make changes, or help a community is by facing and uncovering the truth behind the fears and challenges blocking progress, especially the fears and challenges that are intentionally put there by those in power. It's great if you can band together, when you can work as a team with your friends, unionize, or otherwise organize to tackle an issue from multiple sides, but even if you're going at it alone, showing the Big Bads for the selfish cowards that they are can only help uncover the truth." The Elder sat back.

"And, in the end," said the Vulcan, "however ugly or inconvenient it may be, the truth is all we have."

Live Like a Vulcan

"He lives like a Vulcan," remarked the Hobbit.

"I do," said the Vulcan. "It may be corny to say it would be illogical to live otherwise, but that's the truth. To me, living like a Vulcan doesn't mean being distanced or dispassionate, it means being accepting of life's infinite diversity and infinite combinations. When I was growing up, I felt . . . different. I suppose everyone feels different in their own way, but I think everyone's way of feeling different is unique. I had a great childhood—I was loved, well cared for, and wanted for very little. But, nevertheless, I still felt like an outsider, and Spock helped me understand and appreciate the things that made me feel different. Like Spock, I felt like I was always trying to figure out who I was and how to exist in a world where I didn't seem to completely fit. As a half human growing up on Vulcan, Spock had to find a way to fit in with his all-Vulcan peers, while also acknowledging and reconciling the two parts of himself—the Vulcan side *and* the human side. I may have grown up surrounded by humans," the Vulcan continued, "but I still struggled to blend in and be accepted by my peers without losing touch with the many facets of my own personality. I wanted to watch PBS, not ESPN, but I watched more ball games than I can count because I didn't want to be seen as different. I wanted to stay in my dorm and study, not go out and drink, but I went to the parties to blend in. And all the while I was trying to figure out the difference between who I was, who I wanted to be, and who I *thought* I should be. It was a lot," said the Vulcan.

"It wasn't until I was able to watch and rewatch *Star Trek* on an infinite loop of reruns, tapes, DVDs, and Blu-rays," the Vulcan continued, "that I really allowed myself to see myself as the multifaceted person I am. And then I was able to accept myself for who I was and who I wasn't. I couldn't be the person other people wanted me to be, but I could be the person *I* wanted to be. I also grew to understand and accept the fact that people couldn't be who *I* wanted them to be, either. Spock proved, by joining Starfleet instead of the Vulcan Science Academy, that if others did something or said something I didn't like, I couldn't necessarily argue them into seeing things my way. I didn't have to like them or understand their decisions, but I did have to accept that they weren't going to change just because I wanted them to. This helped me appreciate the differences in other people just as I had learned to appreciate the difference in myself.

"For me, living like a Vulcan means speaking and living my truth. *The* truth—always. Not unkindly, mind you, but a Vulcan knows that it's important to say what you mean and mean what you say, whether it's to your friend or to your superior officer. White lies and misdirection are always options to spare feelings, but they should be used sparingly and with a lot of forethought, and only when simple silence is impossible.

"Part of living like a Vulcan is knowing that relationships are more important than differences. For instance, no Vulcan would go camping for fun. They wouldn't necessarily do many things for *fun*, but if living like a Vulcan means devoting the time and effort to people and experiences you want to have in your life, and your best friends want to sleep under the stars and go rock climbing, why not do it? Living like a Vulcan is about understanding that you don't have to like someone just because you're related to them and it's about understanding the value of true friendship. There was clearly no love lost between Spock and his half-brother, Sybok, but Spock was willing to give his life for the crew of the *Enterprise*. Living like a Vulcan is about doing your duty, trying your best, and being willing to learn more. It's treasuring people and experiences more than possessions. It's about upholding the traditions that mean something to you and forgoing the ones that don't. It's about trusting that your friends will help you through everything from pon farr to daddy issues, and about remembering to center yourself, to enjoy the quiet, and to recharge. It's accepting your and other people's limitations, while always trying to find common ground, peace, and understanding. And it's living a life that at least tries to make the universe a little better than how you found it.

"I live like a Vulcan," the Vulcan concluded, leaning back in his chair, "because, above all else, I want to remain connected to myself, and think that we're all, in many ways, connected to each other."

Love Like a Wookiee

"Connections," the Wookiee said, "that's what it's all about for me. I don't care all that much about things. I mean, things are great—my vintage Death Star playset is still mint-in-box and my signed Peter Mayhew picture hangs above my bed. I love my creature cantina comforts, but I'm a people person under all this fur. For me, it's all about my family, my friends, these guys," the Wookiee said, gesturing to their companions around the table, "and even strangers like you. To paraphrase good ol' Rose Tico, we don't win by defeating what we hate, we win by saving the things we love. Some people think I'm a little ridiculous: Some of my family. Some friends. Pretty much all of my coworkers. But I can't help it, I love like a Wookiee. I may not be as happy to walk around naked like Chewie, but I do know that I have the capacity to love as fully and unconditionally as he did. You see it in *Episode Three* . . ."

I remembered what we'd just discussed about letting people like what they like and kept my prequel opinions to myself.

". . . when Chewie and Yoda stood together on Kashyyyk, first against the droid army and then against the murderous clone army.

The Wookiees loved their home, their planet, and their way of life enough to fight against unimaginable odds to protect it all, but, as the tide turned, though he could have tried to dissuade him from leaving, Chewie loved and respected Yoda enough to let him go. You see it later, too, in the way Chewie loved Han like a brother, repeatedly throwing himself in harm's way to protect him. And though he would have loved Leia because Han did, Chewie truly loved and admired her in his own right. And then you see it again in the way that his love grew to include and envelop Ben. Luke and Lando loved Chewie as much as he loved them, and though the Wookiee didn't show the most sportsmanlike behavior, he loved and protected the droids as best he could. In the final films of *The Skywalker Saga*, his love grew even more to include Rey, Finn, and Poe. And the Maker knows Maz loved him," the Wookiee said wistfully.

"The moments that hit the hardest for me," the Vulcan interjected, "were how evident Chewie's love was during the moments of loss. The way he reacted to Han's death by lashing out at Kylo, but especially how he completely dissolved when he heard about Leia."

"I know," the Wookiee said. "It was heartbreaking. But it's the risk of losing love, the inevitable grief that comes when it's gone, that makes it even more special. As happy as Chewie was to be given Han's Yavin medal, you know he would have given anything for just a few more moments with any of them.

"At the end of the day, through all of the movies, all of the books and the comics, and even the holiday special, which I loved, Wookiees loved what they were all fighting for: freedom, home, family, their past, and everyone's future. All of it. It's all true."

Laugh Like a Hobbit

The Hobbit's smile turned thoughtful. "You know," he said, leaning his elbows on the table and staring at his beer, "all my life, people have called me an optimist. A happy-go-lucky guy who refuses to see life as anything but one big party. I'm there with a big appetite at every meal. I'm always up for a night out, a quick drink, a spontaneous afternoon matinee of a movie I've seen a hundred times before. But if you want to know the truth, I'm not an optimist," the Hobbit admitted. "Not at all. I'm a realist. Like a Hobbit who somehow found himself farther away from home than he'd ever been before, I'm constantly marveling at where I am and how I got here. I think we all do that, at some point, to some degree. I mean, everyone who's ever gone back to their old elementary school or visited their childhood bedroom after they moved away thinks it all looks smaller, right? Your experiences will always shape and change things in the rearview mirror.

"And whether you're physically far from where you started or not, growing up takes you away, emotionally. Life shows you things. Some you've heard about, others you can't imagine. Some of it will be as grand as Rivendell, and some of it will be as terrifying as Shelob's Lair. But all of it is there, waiting for you, one way or another. One minute you're having a pint and setting off fireworks at a picnic, and the next, you're having a pint and trying to stay alive in a pub. Uncertainty is lying in wait for you around every corner. Uncertainty and, let's face it, death. Which is exactly why I try to laugh like a Hobbit: because if you don't laugh, if you don't take the time to enjoy your breakfast, or your second breakfast, if you don't make the effort to hang out with your friends while you can, there's absolutely no guarantee you're going to have the chance to do it again. I laugh like a Hobbit when I find out something I didn't know before, like the fact that trees actually do talk to one another. I laugh when I relax after a job well done because I'm genuinely pleased with myself. I laugh when people who think they're better than me lord their accomplishments over my head, because I know it really cuts them down to size. I laugh at my own mistakes, when I've made too much noise, or when I didn't follow the GPS directions like I should have. I laugh when I find an Arkenstone-like treasure, or even when I just find my keys, because I can't believe I lost them. Again."

The Hobbit laughed as the waiter set a plate of nachos in front of him.

"And I laugh because I'm grateful to have food in my belly. I laugh after a long journey, when I can take the time to reflect on it all, and I laugh when I share the stories with my friends and family out of the sheer joy of being alive at the end of it. I laugh at my friends' weddings and birthday parties because milestones should be celebrated even more than deaths and goodbyes are solemnized. I laugh like a Hobbit because I know that there's darkness out in the world, and the only thing that can keep it from taking over is the rebellious act of joy."

"How we face death is at least as important as how we face life."

—*Star Trek II: The Wrath of Khan*

"**S**orry," said the Hobbit as he shoveled nachos into his mouth. "Didn't mean to take us down a dark road."

"Not at all," said the Elder. "But it does get one thinking about death, doesn't it?"

"I'm never not thinking about it," I admitted.

The Elder placed his hand gently on my shoulder. "Well, that seems a waste of time. Death, as we've seen over and over again in pop culture, is not necessarily the end."

"Force ghosts!" exclaimed the Wookiee.

"Yes!" the Elder agreed. "But even more than that. As Luke Skywalker said, 'No one's ever really gone.' I think he was right. People don't necessarily reappear as ghosts, like the Dead Men of Dunharrow who helped defeat Sauron's forces—"

"He said 'forces'!" interrupted the Wookiee.

"Um, yes. Sometimes, like Loki or Philippa Georgiou, they can die (or not) a few times and then come back from or into a different timeline or universe. Or they're mostly dead, like Westley before Miracle Max and Valerie brought him back, or Spock before landing on Genesis, or even Gandalf going from Grey to White. But, ultimately, characters and stories are kept alive by the ones who remember them. Generations of Jedi and Sith and Man and Dwarf and Klingon live on in the memories of their descendants. They're remembered in the holograms and books and data feeds that they made. They're stored in memory banks and, perhaps more importantly, memorialized in the good that they've left behind. As long as someone is remembered, they're still alive.

"And to get a little meta," the Elder continued, "that goes for the creators of the things we love, too. Just as Leia would never really be gone in the minds of the fictional members of the Rebellion or the Resistance, Carrie Fisher will live on in the hearts of the fans who continue to watch the *Star Wars* movies. Roy Batty will probably be rattling around in some Tyrell computer way beyond 2049, but generations of viewers are going to watch Rutger Hauer talk about tears in the rain forever. Spock is mourned in two timelines just as much as Leonard Nimoy is missed, and celebrated, in this one.

"Let's face it, you have to live your life like it's its own stand-alone movie or TV series. Each person is really just a spin-off from their parents' own shows. There may be multiple episodes, but it's a one-and-done season. And sure, you could conceivably be part of a reboot in which you remake yourself after mistakes or recast your life with other people, but you're never going to escape cancellation by the big network in the sky. Take Frasier: he started as a guest character on *Cheers*, became a regular, then got his own show where he reinvented himself. But eventually, even he was canceled. It's because of books and audio and video and storytelling that characters and creators and films and shows live on. But most importantly, because of memory, no one is ever really gone. You keep your friends and family alive as reruns in your heart and your mind. And you'll be kept alive in the hearts and minds of those you leave behind."

"And life isn't like most video games, where you can relive life after life after life. It's more like *Oregon Trail*—it's just a matter of time before we get dysentery!" the Hobbit mused.

"It can be so hard, though," I said. "Sometimes loss is just too much to bear."

The Elder put his hand on my shoulder. "Of course, it can be. And it can feel that way for a long while. So much has been said and written about coping with the loss of a loved one, but I think what Vision said to Wanda may be my favorite."

The Wookiee looked up, remembering. "Vision said, 'What is grief if not love persevering?'"

The Elder nodded. "What are we supposed to do with the love we hold for someone when they're not there anymore? It can be devastating. It often is. And I think, as we've seen in characters from Wanda to Leia to John Wick, that grief may never go away, but it can change into, hopefully, something less painful. Maybe something that you can eventually smile about."

"The trick," the Hobbit said after we sat silently for a few moments, "when you're trying to get through any difficulty is to 'just keep swimming! Just keep swimming!'" He looked at the Elder. "See," he said, "I can quote movies, too!"

The Wookiee pointed their furry arm toward the door. "And Dory is right! The only way to get around a problem is to get through it. That's how you make the Kessel Run in less than twelve parsecs."

"It really should be *fewer* than," the Vulcan corrected.

"That quote's canon," said the Wookiee.

"It's always bugged me," sighed the Vulcan.

The Wookiee shrugged their shoulders. "But Frogger never stopped trying to get across the street, did he? Lara Croft never stopped going on adventures despite not knowing what she'd find. With everything going on out there," they said, "I refuse to give up hope. I don't think any of us can afford to do that."

"Hope? What's there to hope about?" I asked.

The Wookiee leaned their furry elbows on the table. "Anything. Everything! There's so much to hope for! Our being here tonight in these cosplays proves that we believe in the power of hope. Look at me: Leia may have said Obi-Wan was her only hope in *A New Hope*, and she was disappointed when she didn't get any responses to her distress calls on the way to Crait in *The Last Jedi*, but it was her hope in the Rebellion and the Resistance, and the hope her friends had in her, that got them through it all." They pointed to the Hobbit. "The Fellowship of the Ring would never have succeeded if any of its members had given up hope of Frodo and Sam making it to Mount Doom." They tilted their head toward the Vulcan. "And heck, the entirety of *Star Trek*, the Federation, and Starfleet is built on the hope of all of humanity and the universe working together toward a future of equality and prosperity." We all nodded in agreement. "You roll the dice in Dungeons & Dragons hoping you'll be able to strike a hit. Comic books, novels, movies, TV shows, and heck, even sports—if that's your thing—are all motivated by the idea of hope: Hope in success. Hope in good winning over bad. Hope for a happy ending. Without hope, there is just no imaginative engine to propel anything forward; there's no future. Hope is one of the things we can cling to and, at the same time, share and give away."

The Elder smiled. "It's as renewable a resource as life, love, and laughter."

I think the Wookiee smiled in return. "And it's right here, right now. Not in a galaxy far, far away, or a far distant future, or even in Middle-earth."

I raised my glass. "I'd like to make a toast." The others raised their own glasses. "To hope!"

"To hope!"

"To hope!"

"To hope!"

"To hope!"

"I found the seer's body in the quicksand."

—Krull

I was amazed at how thoughtful and easy everyone was together. "I wish I could do what you're doing," I said to no one in particular.

"Eat without getting it all over our clothes?" asked the Vulcan.

"No," I said, looking at the mess I'd made on my shirt and wondering when I'd eaten . . . was that hummus? "No, no, I mean cosplay. I could never do that."

"Why not?" asked the Hobbit. "It's just a matter of buying the right things . . ."

"Or making it yourself," offered the Wookiee.

"It's not that," I said. "Well, I'm not very skilled with a needle and thread, so I would have to buy it all." The Hobbit sat a little taller in his seat. "I just don't think I could pull it off."

"It's really nothing," said the Wookiee. "You just have to inhale and give it a good tug. And honestly, you usually wind up so sweaty by the end of the day that it all comes off pretty easily. But if you're wearing a lot of pleather or latex, you may have to peel everything off instead of tugging."

"I mean, I don't think I could get away with it," I said. "I'm too uncoordinated to walk around in a big costume without bumping into everything, and I don't have the right body for anything tight-fitting. People would think I look stupid."

"Quicksand!" exclaimed the Elder.

"What?" I asked, partly because I wondered where the Elder was going with this line of thought, and also because I wondered if the glob on my shirt *wasn't* hummus, but maybe some sort of cream-based soup?

"Pop culture taught us that quicksand is an ever-present danger," the Elder explained. "Take one false step and then, boom, you'll find yourself ankle-, then knee-, then hip-deep in the stuff. Struggling only makes it worse, doesn't it? Before you know it, it's up to your elbows and your shoulders. You try to remain calm, but soon you can't raise your arms anymore, and when you scream for help, it starts flowing into your mouth and ears. And then the last thing you see before it takes you fully under is just more sand, until it stings your eyes with its gritty, blinding sharpness, and then you're suffocated. Crushed under the weight of tons of sand. Quicksand isn't something you get out of." I looked at the Elder nervously, wondering if this story was going to get less bleak.

"Swamps are dangerous, too, but those at least offer the possibility of escape," the Elder continued. "Swamps have bottoms, however muddy they may be, to walk along if you can hold your breath for long enough. And the trees, vines, and other plants that grow out of and around swamps could, if you're close enough, give you something to hold on to so you don't sink down any farther, or help you pull yourself out, just like how Westley and Buttercup escaped from the Fire Swamp in *The Princess Bride.*

"But be careful not to count on the flowers and fauna around the swamp *too* much. Some of them, like a Venus flytrap or an Audrey II, will keep their jaws open, waiting and biding their time, until an unsuspecting insect alights inside their poisonous maw and then, at just the right moment, clamps its jaw shut, capturing the doomed victim until its body is slowly, fully, and, I would imagine, painfully dissolved. And then, once nothing remains of the kill, the carnivorous flower living at the edge of a swamp again opens its mouth, waiting for the next feeding time. But like the handholds that rise up from swamps, nature has given the potential victims of these plants—these real-life mean green mothers—some help. Because it's during those in-between times, the times when a bug or dentist or flower shop proprietor is trapped, that other potential victims are given a fighting chance for survival. They can readily see their trapped, semi-digested friends as a warning, and have the opportunity to just keep flying along or take the train somewhere else that's green." Like a coyote clinging to a cliff, I strained to hold on to the hope that this conversation would get less bleak.

"Swamps are dangerous," said the Elder. "But quicksand? Quicksand's the worst. There's nothing growing out of it. Nothing to hold on to. There's no escape from quicksand. Unless, of course, a person standing far enough away can toss you something to hold on to, like Mutt throwing a snake to Indy when he was sinking. But the chances of anyone getting that close, or even close enough to hear your screams, are slim to none. And though Rey, Poe, Finn, Chewie, and the droids made their way through the quicksand of Pasaana into a hidden cavern below, the bottom of a quicksand pit is usually packed with sand and the mummified bodies of the poor souls who sank. Unless you're on a planet like Arrakis, where the sand's fine but the giant sandworms are gonna get ya." I picked another bit of food off my shirt and rolled it between my fingers, the thought of sand stuck to my mind. It felt too gritty to be hummus. Maybe a stone-ground mustard? I hate gritty foods. It's the sandy texture that gets me. Like Anakin, I hate sand. Whether it's on Arrakis or Tatooine or Vulcan or Coney Island, it's just the worst. I've told my family that neither I nor any of my things should be buried in the sand or I'd come back and Force ghost–haunt them till they died.

"And unlike swamps that have plants and trees and mud surrounding it, quicksand offers no warning to passersby," the Elder went on. "One minute you're happily walking on a sandy but sturdy-enough ground in a forest, desert, or innocent-looking park, and the next, you're ever-so-slowly sinking toward doom and death. There are no bones, no clothes along the edge to serve as warning. No signs that tell you to go back the way you came from. And there's nothing growing into or out of it to hold on to. Quicksand lays in wait, quietly, contentedly, and completely alone. For you. Which begs the question: When was the *last* time you saw any quicksand?"

We looked at one another and all shook our heads.

"And when was the *first* time you saw quicksand?"

Again, we shook our heads, united in the fact that none of us had ever had any personal experience with the stuff.

"So, unlike swamps, which not only exist in real life but can be relatively easily avoided, quicksand exists, for the most part, in your minds?" the Elder asked. We agreed.

The Elder turned to me. "You say that you think people would make fun of you for wearing a costume. That your body is too ill-suited to wear the kind of clothing you wish. And you think—you truly believe—that despite the hundreds of people walking around and bumping into one another, themselves dressed as any number of elves or aliens or pirates or zombies or spandex-clad heroes . . . you believe that *they* would think less of *you* for doing what *they're* doing? That they would give you as much negative attention as you're giving yourself? I bet you feel the same, more or less, about lots of different social situations. In your mind, you're not walking into a party, going to a restaurant, or even walking down the street; you're stepping right into quicksand. And you find yourself gasping for air, so weighted down by the negativity and judgment of others that you're convinced you will die."

I nodded.

"But the quicksand you fear is not out there," the Elder said, gesturing toward the door, "but in here," he continued, pointing to my head. "Pop culture has warned us that we should watch out for quicksand on any path we take. But rather than being found physically underfoot, the quicksand is actually found on our emotional journeys, when our brains try to smother themselves under the weight of anxiety, uncertainty, and doubt. And it's those suffocating and self-abusive thoughts that we then project outward onto social situations, tricking ourselves into thinking of them as inevitable, fatal dangers."

"It's a metaphor!" shouted the Hobbit.

The Elder continued, "Swamps are as real as any kind of social situation you could conceivably find yourself in," the Elder continued. "And like a swamp, you don't just happen upon a meeting or party. Unlike quicksand, you'll have plenty of warning that you're about to encounter one. And though they can, indeed, be terrifying in their own ways, they're also teeming with life, beauty, and opportunity. Like swamps, some situations are too toxic or too dangerous to enter into, but there are warning signs to help you avoid those situations if you look for them. Do you see an abandoned pair of binoculars or a single bloody boot suspiciously close to the threshold? That's a red flag. Is there an unspoken-but-understood barrier to entry or general bad vibe? Are they being openly discriminatory, cruel, or unkind to people? Turn back—you wouldn't want to be friends with those people in the first place."

The Wookiee raised their hand as if in class. "So rather than believing that we'll find it at every turn, we should recognize quicksand as the very real, but very limited, self-imposed danger that it is?"

"Yes," the Elder agreed. "Sometimes people just happen to be laughing near you—and not at you."

"Unless you're *trying* to make them laugh," interrupted the Hobbit.

"Yes," the Elder agreed. "And sometimes people are admiring your shirt, or your face, not making fun of it. And sometimes—most times—people are too wrapped up worrying about what everyone else thinks about *them* to think about you. In fact, I think you'll find that most of the people you'll ever meet are on the precipice, thinking about how they can avoid falling into the swamp themselves. But when you do find yourself in a swamp—and inevitably you will—those are the people who will throw you a vine or even a snake to help pull you out. And if they find themselves treading water beside you, they're the ones who will work cooperatively with you, like Bastian did for Artax in *The NeverEnding Story*, to help rescue you."

"Ah—but for all Bastian's pulling, coaxing, and crying, Artax died in the Swamp of Sadness," I reminded him.

"Artax was a horse. A fictional horse whose fate was written by some screenwriters and put through lots of focus groups and Hollywood machinery," the Elder replied. "You are a person. A person with free will, the capacity for complex thought, and the use of opposable thumbs. So, if and when you do find yourself in a swamp, remind yourself that you are not an Artax, but instead a Westley and Buttercup, who had the wherewithal to work together to escape the Fire Swamp. And, of course, William Goldman, Rob Reiner, and Norman Lear as guardian studio angels protecting them.

"Avoid unnecessary risks, and protect yourself, but allow yourself at least the option to walk on a beach, a sidewalk, or a convention center floor without worrying about falling deep inside the ground. But do continue to take care around swamps. They're really real. And really terrible."

"Fly casual."

—Star Wars Episode VI: Return of the Jedi

"OK, so let's say you get over your initial fear and decide to do a thing. You go to a party or a job interview or just go to the mall because you really like that one pretzel place in the food court. How do you actually get *through* a situation?" I asked.

The Elder leaned toward me. "What do you mean? You've already done it. You came to this convention alone. You walked into this space alone. You sat with us alone."

"Yeah," I admitted, "but I came to the con already knowing the lay of the land, and to be honest, tonight, I was starving and just assumed I'd eat quickly, and alone, and then run up to my room. I was desperate to do both."

"I never would have known that," the Elder replied kindly. "You walked in here like you were totally comfortable." Had he forgotten about my trouble with the door? "Well, except for not knowing how to open the door." He had not. "It sounds like you watched enough *Star Wars* to learn how to fly casual."

I thought about this for a moment. "You mean like when Han and Chewie had to get the stolen shuttle through the Imperial blockade?"

"Yes," said the Elder. "Han knew they had to make it past that obstacle to complete their mission. So rather than flying straight through or hanging back, each of which would raise suspicions, Han told Chewie to 'fly casual,' meaning just close enough, at just enough speed, without activating the defector shield, to make it seem like they belonged where they were. By tricking the Imperial armada, they were also, in a way, tricking themselves into believing that their scheme would work."

"Ah," said the Hobbit, "the classic 'fake it till you make it' maneuver!"

"But for nerds!" said the Vulcan.

"Just like when Samwise Gamgee saved Frodo by using his own shadow to scare the orcs," said the Hobbit. "They thought he was a giant, hulking threat without ever actually seeing him. Once they were all gone, he was able to get to Frodo without having to actually fight any of them."

"Exactly." The Elder turned back to me. "I never would have guessed that you were uncomfortable or scared."

"I never said scared," I mumbled, trying to convince myself as well as them.

"But because you walked in, after you'd finally figured out how to open the door that is, you gave off an air of surety and purpose, and I bet you began to believe it yourself. Even for just a moment."

"I suppose you're right," I admitted. "I guess I did start to believe I could walk past all these tables without bumping into them."

"And not only did I think that you should be here, I thought you thought it, too. Just fly casual," the Elder said, patting my shoulder, "and you've got it made."

Go, Speed Round, Go!

"This is all fascinating, but I don't think you could cite a lesson from every single bit of pop culture."

The Vulcan, Wookiee, and Hobbit all stopped eating and looked at the Elder.

"Try me," he said, as they all leaned back in their seats and exchanged knowing smiles.

"OK," I said. "I'll name a movie or show or character and you give me a lesson."

"Let's do this," the Elder replied, sitting a little straighter in his seat.

Now that I recognized how to fly casual, I sat up straighter, too, and found myself genuinely excited for the volley. "Let's start with video games. *Pac-Man*."

"You'll never outrun your ghosts, so face them."

"*Ms. Pac-Man*."

"A woman's place is anywhere she wants to be."

"*Donkey Kong*."

"Skilled tradespeople deserve just as much respect as the college-educated."

"*Q*bert.*"

"Why walk when you can hop?"

"*Animal Crossing.*"

"Vegetarianism shouldn't be mocked."

"*Tomb Raider.*"

"Destroy the patriarchy."

"*Minecraft.*"

"We learn by exploring."

"*Fortnite.*"

"Evolve or die."

"*Halo.*"

"Little good can come from colonialism."

"*Grand Theft Auto.*"

"Sometimes it feels good to be bad."

"*Final Fantasy.*"

"Nothing's ever really final."

I threw my hands in the air as the others cheered the Elder.

"Well played. Next time we're doing superheroes. But in the meantime," I said as the waiter approached, "this round's on me!"

"There is a clause in the contract."

—Alien

The waiter asked if we were staying at the hotel. I said I was because I got a good rate, a voucher for a free breakfast, and since I booked my reservation during a promotion, the hotel would donate a portion of the proceeds to a charity. "That's pretty generous," I said.

"Oh, please," said the waiter. "If the hotel was actually generous, they'd make sure everyone who works here was paid better than minimum wage. I know a lot of people who work at the hotel. From the people at the reception desk to the folks who clean up the rooms. Most of them really like what they do and want to do a good job, but would it kill the hotel bigwigs to pay their CEO less and the boots-on-the-ground workers a little more so they wouldn't have to work so much overtime or get second jobs to make ends meet?"

I was speechless. "Don't worry, man," he said. "That's just corporate America! I'll be back in a minute with your drinks."

"Ugh, I hope I didn't upset him," I worried.

"I'm sure not, but it sort of proves that the Weyland-Yutani approach to management is alive and well!" remarked the Elder.

"The company from *Alien*?" I asked.

"That one. I think *Alien* taught us many important lessons. First of all, they were right—no one can hear you scream in space. Second, it's important to learn the Heimlich maneuver. And third, for the most part, corporations do not care about their employees as much as they say they do. Time and time again, Weyland-Yutani was focused on their singular goals to bring back and weaponize the Xenomorphs."

"I think in *Prometheus*, Weyland was trying to live forever . . . or something?" I asked. The film had always confused me.

"Possibly. That film confuses me," said the Elder, validating my concerns. "But had they, at any time, put their employees' health and safety before their profits or whatever it was they thought would help The Company, the first movie would have been twenty minutes long. The Company even intentionally programmed robots to lie, cheat, and steal their way around the humans. In fact, they were very clear, when Ripley woke up from her nap, that they held her responsible for the loss of money, and *then* it was, 'Oh by the way you've been asleep for years and your daughter's dead.'

"And the list of evil corporations in pop culture goes on and on: Remember Initech from *Office Space*? Their soul-crushing busywork and bureaucracy drove their employees to madness! Buy-n-Large only wanted to sell, sell, sell without any real concern for humanity or the earth until WALL-E and EVE upended everything. And can we pause for a moment to remember the hundreds of people who were killed by the maleficence of Jurassic Park and InGen? They keep opening up the park and convincing people to come!" exclaimed the Elder.

"Ooh, ooh! I have one," said the Vulcan, raising his hand. "The Umbrella Corporation! That's kind of Big Pharma at its worst, right?"

"The Soylent Corporation!" I added. "They tricked people into eating other people!"

"Skynet!" said the Wookiee.

"*Actually*, the name of the company was Cyberdyne Systems," corrected the Hobbit. "Skynet was just a computer system."

The Wookiee cocked their head. "OK, nerd, you do one."

The Hobbit thought for a moment. "*Blade Runner*'s Tyrell Corporation. Sure, let's make robots that could go crazy, but we'll make them so easily outdated that they'll need to be replaced every few years, so maybe nobody will notice."

That was a good one.

"I think we can all agree," said the Elder, "that even though the laws of man allow for a corporation to be considered a person, corporations usually have no humanity."

"Hire the clown."

—The Dark Knight

"Speaking of which," said the Vulcan, "have you ever noticed that you can often tell that something's evil just by what they're called or where they are?"

"What do you mean?" asked the Wookiee.

"Well, for example, you've got the Justice League or the Legion of Superheroes or The Avengers or even The Defenders. They just sound good, right? But then you've also got the Sinister Six and the Legion of Doom and the Injustice League. I mean, it's kind of putting a hat on a hat. Nobody thinks a trip to the Hall of Doom is going to be as uplifting as one to the Hall of Justice. Nobody thinks Mount Doom or an abandoned amusement park or chemical factory would make as great a shared office space as a floor in Avengers Tower or the Baxter Building. And if you name your ship Birds of Prey or Star Destroyers or, heck, Death Star, you're kind of signaling that you're up to no good, right?

"And, come on," the Vulcan continued, "if you *choose* to call yourself Cruella or Maleficent or Doctor Doom or Evil-Lyn rather than, say, Blossom, Bubbles, or Buttercup, you're not making the best first impression—and you're really giving the people at the DMV a lot to talk about. If you work with a group called the Death Eaters or the Brotherhood of Evil Mutants or the Red Lanterns, you're going to wind up with fewer endorsements on LinkedIn than you would if you're working for Aperture Science or Fontaine Futuristics. And if you intentionally name your child something like 'Mr. Sinister,' 'Stompa,' or 'Karen,' their charisma points have already taken a pretty big hit before they've even had a chance to roll their own dice."

Go, Speed Round, Go Go!

"**R**eady for a superhero speed round?" I asked.

"Ready!" exclaimed the Elder. I was glad to see he was having as much fun as I was.

"Aquaman."

"Don't let other people's impressions of you dictate who you really are."

"Black Panther."

"Be the role model you wished you had when you were young."

"Spider-Man, and don't give me the 'With great power comes great responsibility' line."

"Youthful exuberance should not be seen as a negative."

"That'll do. Thor."

"With great privilege comes great responsibility. Be worthy of it."

"I'll allow it. Ant-Man."

"Size has no bearing on ability."

"The X-Men."

"Representation matters."

"Loki."

"Use your power for good. But there's nothing wrong with a little mischief."

"Iron Fist."

"Cultural appropriation and whitewashing have never really been okay, and are completely unacceptable in the twenty-first century."

"Mr. Fantastic."

"You won't always have the answer."

"Black Widow."

"Immigrants make this country great."

"Captain Marvel."

"Which one?"

"Good question. Marvel."

"Respect women. And the armed services."

"DC's Captain Marvel, though I must remind you that he's now just called 'Shazam.'"

"Whatever. He'll always be Captain Marvel to me. Children should be seen *and* heard."

"Superman."

"Everyone has a weakness."

"Batman."

"Everyone has pain they carry with them every day."

"I'm done!" I exclaimed, slumping down in my seat and extending my hand to congratulate the Elder on another victory. "Next up, classic TV."

"There is no good and evil."

—Harry Potter and the Sorcerer's Stone

"Can we talk about evil monsters for a second?" asked the Hobbit. We all agreed to move the subject of conversation along. "And how most of them aren't really evil? Sure, some of them are, but most of the ones in movies aren't that bad, really. Take Frankenstein . . ."

"You mean 'Frankenstein's monster.' Boy, I hate it when people think the name of the monster is Frankenstein," said the Wookiee.

"No, I *meant* Frankenstein. *The doctor.* I think he's the true monster of the whole story. Heck, he didn't even give the monster a name, so we all have to call him Frankenstein's monster!" replied the Hobbit.

The Wookiee nodded in agreement. "It's true. We do."

"So Frankenstein's monster is made up of lots of other dead people," the Hobbit continued. "He didn't want to be reborn, but he was. A few stitches, a few operations, and a bolt of lightning later and—ZAP—he's alive, and doesn't know where he is, who he is, or what the heck's going on. All he wants is to figure it all out, but the next thing he knows, he's being chased by idiots with pitchforks who don't like him because they think he's an abomination. All he wanted to do was live his life—the life he was forced back into! It's not fair.

"Dracula?" the Hobbit went on. "I'd be in a bad mood, too, if I was vitamin D deficient and hangry, so cut him some slack. The Creature from the Black Lagoon? Poor thing's just swimming around, minding his own business, and all of a sudden people want to poke and prod him for no good reason. Witches may want to nibble on a kid every once in a while, but let's face it, they're hunted because the patriarchy fears them. The Mummy's sleeping for centuries when a bunch of colonizers wake him up. Would *you* be in a good mood without any coffee? I could go on," said the Hobbit.

"Please do!" I exclaimed. I was enjoying this monologue too much for him to stop.

"Fine! Werewolves want, like, one night a month to go out and party. Is that too much to ask? Sure, the Invisible Man may have gone a little overboard, but all he really wanted was to do science. Zombies used to be people—they didn't choose to be mindless mind eaters, so how about treating them with a little respect and taking the kill shot without a lot of needless flourish to prove how big of a living man you are? The Phantom of the Opera had a really bad accident and just wants to be left alone with a piano. Quasimodo is tortured by everyone because of the way he looks and just wants to live as normal a life as possible without being killed.

"Most of the monsters in movies are metaphors—yes, more metaphors!—for the emotions that we, as people, feel all the time. Every day. And the only difference is that they look or sound different or come from a different place or can't communicate in a language that other people can understand. Most of them aren't inherently bad, they just have big emotions and feelings and are misunderstood. The only true monsters are people. PEOPLE! If we all stopped to consider that maybe we're misunderstanding or misinterpreting other people's actions as evil or bad when they're really just feeling big emotions, and may not be able to express them, or acknowledge that we can feel big emotions ourselves, and may not always have the right language or tools or ability to express them, we may finally see that there are more people than monsters in the world. In fact, there are no monsters! There are only people! Can . . . can I stop now?" the Hobbit asked, out of breath.

"Yes!" we said, applauding, as he drained his beer mug.

"And I would add," said the Elder, "that everyone is the hero in their own story."

I nodded in agreement. "Yeah. I mean, Magneto had some pretty good points. Killmonger did, too," I said. "Lots of supervillains have these lofty goals but go about achieving them in a terrible way."

The Hobbit bristled a little. "You can't tell me every supervillain is really a good guy?"

"Oh no no no," I said. "But I think there's a huge difference between a bad guy like Darkseid, who wants to control everything, and someone like Lex Luthor, who in his own twisted way is trying to save humanity." The Vulcan seemed unconvinced. "I'm not saying villains are justified in doing what they do, but some of them at least start in a more benign place. At the end of the day—or in this case the 'dark night'"—I paused for a moment, very satisfied with my pun—"Poison Ivy kills men because they're harming the planet and she's an environmentalist at heart. Sybok genuinely thought he was trying to find and save God. Thanos wanted to kill half the universe not to punish them but to save the other half. They were all the heroes in their own stories and did what they did for what they saw as the greater good."

The Vulcan considered what I'd said. "And I suppose there are some villains who see the error of their ways and turn good. There's more to them than black and white. There's a reason charts go from Lawful Good to Chaotic Evil."

"Yes!" I agreed. "In the comics, the Riddler was, for a while at least, a great detective who was able to solve mysteries that gave even Batman trouble. Loki's switched sides more times than he could count, and though he's usually just in it for himself, he's still got his own brand of familial loyalty and responsibility. Harley Quinn may be the greatest example of an antihero. She's arguably one of the most loved and cosplayed characters of all time, and she's only been around since 1992! Catwoman, the Punisher, Electra—are they good? Bad? Who can say? Like anyone with access to the right support and resources, they have the chance to learn and grow from their mistakes—if, that is, they see their past misdeeds as mistakes at all."

The Hobbit slouched in his chair. "But some people won't do that. They won't learn from their mistakes. Some people insist on making them over and over again. Some people are just . . . bad."

"But I don't think that most people want to be," said the Elder, patting the Hobbit's shoulder. "It goes back to what we were saying before about hope. I hope that the people who do bad things are doing them not because they were born evil, but because they're hurt or scared or somehow in great need of something. Love, maybe? Understanding? Compassion?"

"Hunger?" offered the Hobbit with a sly smile.

"Yes. Mr. Freeze steals to save his wife. Wanda took over Westview because she was under the weight of unspeakable grief. Gollum was driven mad by the Ring. Snape killed Dumbledore as a mercy. You never know what someone is going through, and you never know the lengths they'll be pushed to as a result." The Elder paused for a long moment and stared at his glass as if lost in a memory. "And you never know how you yourself will react until you're in a given situation. The best we can hope for, the most we can do for each other, is to try to remember that we're all the heroes in our own stories."

"Unless they admit to being a villain!" said the Hobbit, trying to bring the Elder back.

The Elder smiled. "Well, if they're going to admit it, then send them into the abyss!"

He paused for a moment, considering something. "We see that same humanity in the actual superheroes, too: time and again, pop culture shows us that it's not a character's superpowers that matter—what matters is how their humanity shapes their use of those powers."

"Yeah," said the Hobbit. "Superman is only truly super because of the way he was raised and the values instilled in him. Tony Stark isn't heroic just because he wears a suit; he's heroic because he cares about people. T'Challa's physical strength may come from heart-shaped herbs, but it's his desire to do right by and for his people that makes him great. Sam and Merry and Pippin didn't possess a powerful ring, but they still sacrificed everything to help their friend and save their homes. Finn didn't need the Force to do the right thing, and Picard was heroic because of the ideals and principles he believed in. You don't need a spider bite or a chemical bath or super serum or even trillions of dollars to be a hero. You need a moral compass and a support system."

"And a willingness to fail," added the Vulcan. "Time and time again we've seen that if a hero is overconfident, they'll fail. Poe didn't stop to consider he could be wrong before trying to mutiny against Holdo. But he was. He didn't stop to think that he didn't have all the information. He just thought he knew best. Star-Lord thought Thanos couldn't break free from Doctor Strange, Spider-Man, Iron Man, Mantis, and the others, but he did. And then he snapped half the universe away. It's when heroes think there's a chance of losing that they're at their best, because despite that, they still try. The odds were against man, Hobbit, elf, and dwarf during the battles of Helm's Deep and the Five Armies, and against the Rebels on Scarif and the Resistance on Crait. And to say nothing of the no-win situation faced by generations of Starfleet officers during the Kobayashi Maru simulations! Kirk famously never believed in a no-win situation, so it's lucky for him that he had Spock and Bones as sounding boards. Ultimately, what makes a hero a hero is their willingness to try to do the right thing."

"Punishment means nothing to them."

—A Clockwork Orange

T he Wookiee took a sip from their glass. "You know, speaking of 'good and evil,' there's one thing that's always stood out to me in comic books . . ."

"Just one thing?" joked the Hobbit.

"Well, the biggest one, I guess, is the whole *idea* of the bad guy. Or girl. Or robot. Whatever—you get what I'm saying. The way that quote, unquote 'bad' android, alien, or wizard is dealt with after their evil schemes are thwarted. I mean, if you take a look at, say, Superman's villains, or even Wonder Woman's, or the Flash's, for the most part, they're all, well, bad people. They may have specific character traits and motivations, but the vast majority of them are just criminals or evil geniuses: Lex Luthor's driven mostly by his hatred of Superman, and every time he gets caught, he's sent back to jail. Or elected president, but that's another story. And because they're calculating and know what they're doing is wrong, General Zod and other Kryptonians are sent to the Phantom Zone, rather than sent to therapy. Ares is the god of war so that's kind of all he does and suffers punishments suitable for gods, like banishment or imprisonment in a labyrinth or whatever. Gorilla Grodd wants to subjugate humankind, and when he's defeated, he's sent back to Gorilla City for justice to be meted out by a jury of his peers. You get the idea—the bad get caught and, as a consequence of their actions, must then pay their debts to society.

"But a lot of Batman's villains are 'bad' because of their mental illnesses," said the Wookiee. "Some of them, like Poison Ivy or Cat-woman, are thrown into Blackgate Prison, which makes sense because Ivy's a terrorist and Selina Kyle's a thief, but an awful lot of them are sent to Arkham Asylum, which makes sense: The Joker is a sociopath. Harley may be an antihero, but she's clearly suffering from a love addiction or some sort of obsession with the Joker. Two-Face suffers from dissociative identity disorder. The Mad Hatter's delusional. The years of mental torture Killer Croc received because of his physical differences surely damaged him. And, let's face it, Batman's suffering from severe PTSD, multiple obsessions and compulsions, and some form of hero complex, all stemming from his parents' deaths.

"A lot of these criminals aren't just sent to prison, they're sent to Arkham Asylum to be treated by doctors who are, at least in theory, there to help them. I mean, sometimes they're sent to jail, or to both jail *and* Arkham, but there's at least a recognition in these villains' stories that they are mentally ill and not necessarily completely responsible for their actions. They're not perfect models by any means, but I think comics have at least tried to show the effects mental illness has on individuals, families, and societies. Every choice a person makes has its own consequences. But illness requires treatment and help, not punishment."

"Backstory stuff."

—The Lego Movie

"I usually let the Wookiee win, but in this case, they do have a valid point," said the Vulcan.

"There are so many reboots and sequels out there these days. Creators are always going back to the well to tell stories in new or different ways, but I think one of the more interesting trends has been the backstory prequel."

"I dunno," said the Hobbit gravely. "Sometimes prequels do more harm than good, especially when they're not well thought out or done as a money grab."

"He's right," I said. "I always respond better to a prequel if there's a reason for it."

"Agreed," said the Vulcan. "Doing a prequel based on a one-line or passing reference in something is a stretch. And doing one that tries to correct too many plot holes or clean up loose ends is dangerous, too." He looked pointedly at the Wookiee.

"Why are you looking at me?" they said.

"No reason," replied the Vulcan. "But I'm reminded of all the prequels that try to justify what characters did in the movies or stories where we first met them."

"Try?" I asked.

"All of them *try*," he replied, "and many succeed. But whether it's *Solo* or *Maleficent* or Glenn Close's *Dalmatian* movies, or even the *X-Men: First Class* prequel trilogy, they each show younger, perhaps greener and more naïve, versions of the characters that we know and love, or at least know and love to hate. Timeline shuffling and plot holes aside, I think the main thing I've learned—that we've all learned—is that everybody has their own backstory."

The Vulcan nodded to me. "For example, the only things I really know about you are the things that we've talked about here. You've lived a whole life that I don't know about. You could have that haircut because you had a terrible experience with a barber as a child for all I know."

"Wait, what?" I said, feeling around my head for a cowlick or something.

"We all have our own backstories," the Vulcan continued, unconcerned about my mild panic. "Our poor waiter could be the heir to a Stark-like fortune. This Wookiee may be keeping their giant furry head on because they're wanted by the police."

"I'm . . . I'm not," they replied.

"Hey, you never know. None of us ever know. Spock himself had a backstory and he never even told Kirk or Bones about it. He had a half-brother? A stepsister? Gandalf had hundreds of years of adventures and tragedy that he kept to himself. Heck, Bilbo never told Frodo or anyone else about his adventures with the dwarfs and Gandalf. Did any of us know, when we first saw Darth Vader, that he started out as a little blond kid with a knack for pod racing and droid building? We all have backstories. Did any of us know that Maleficent was betrayed by Aurora's father? No, we just thought she was annoyed she wasn't invited to a party. Did we immediately clock Aragorn as the heir to the crown? Nope, he was just the brooding hottie in the corner. If we hadn't known that the Kelvin Universe Spock was one of the last of his species, we would have hated him for even thinking about leaving Starfleet.

"Some of us have good backstories, some bad, some worse than we could imagine," said the Vulcan. "And just like how everyone's the hero of their own story, knowing that we really don't know anyone until we, well, *know* them, I think the only thing we can do is to be kind. You never know who just sorted into a lousy House, who lost a land war in China, or who just endured a really bad commute to their office in downtown Los Santos."

"What if they work from home?" asked the Hobbit.

The Vulcan leaned forward and stared into his eyes. "Then maybe they didn't have enough coffee. Which is, as Captain Janeway proved, the absolute worst thing that could happen. Ever."

"Assemble!"

—*Avengers: Endgame*

"**A**ll that being said, even if you do know someone's backstory, that doesn't mean you have to like them, or excuse them for bad behavior," said the Vulcan, leaning back.

"Totally," said the Hobbit. "But it's amazing what can happen to relationships when you're forced together, isn't it? Kind of like how Brody, Quint, and Hooper learned to work together in *Jaws*, pop culture is filled with unlikely team-ups, teams made up of people who didn't like each other, or teams that could only be brought together under just the right set of circumstances. But, in the end, it all kind of works. Nick Fury assembled the original Avengers not because they could work together but because they *had* to work together. Even though Thor and Tony fought the first time they met, and Cap and Tony had a huge number of differences, they all grew to respect each other. Each member of the Justice League has their own way of doing things, but they all came together for a common purpose. Who could have thought that Klingons would join the Federation, or that the Flintstones could ever meet the Jetsons? And who would have guessed that a Fellowship made up of a dwarf, an elf, two men, a wizard, and four Hobbits could ever have saved the world? Gimli and Legolas had generations of racial prejudice to get around."

"Racial? Maybe 'special'?" I asked.

"Could be," said the Vulcan. Or 'specious'? Whatever it was, there was a lot of deep-seated stuff between them, and don't forget that Boromir was always on the verge of killing Frodo. Did Iron Man ever really forgive Doctor Strange for giving up his Infinity Stone? Could Renee Montoya ever truly forgive Harley for all of the bad stuff she did before they joined together as the Birds of Prey? Who knows, but they all either looked past their issues or at least temporarily forgot about their bad blood in order to band together to get the job done."

I saw where he was going with this. "Who would have thought that Kong and Godzilla would ever work together? But if they didn't get over their own issues, Mechagodzilla would have become Earth's new alpha predator. They fought, then worked together, then just agreed to disagree and left each other in peace."

"Precisely. You don't have to like the people you work with," said the Vulcan, "but you do have to at least respect the positive things they bring to the table."

Go, Speed Round, Go Go Go!

'd been itching to challenge the Elder again.

"Are you ready for another speed round?" I asked.

"You shall not pass," he said, pushing up his sleeves.

"*Bewitched.*"

"No relationship is without its secrets."

"*I Dream of Jeannie.*"

"Any relationship between adults is fine if it's consensual."

"*The Addams Family.*"

"Every family is weird in its own way."

"*The Munsters.*"

"Beauty is relative."

"*The Muppet Show.*"

"Inclusion and diversity are assets to any organization."

"*The Flintstones.*"

"Technology and modern conveniences are luxuries to be appreciated."

"*The Jetsons.*"

"Technology and modern conveniences are no substitute for real-life personal interaction and connection."

"The Road Runner and Wile E. Coyote."

"Watch what people do, not what they say. Especially if they never say anything other than calling themselves a 'Super Genius.'"

"*Tom and Jerry.*"

"Violence is never the answer."

"*Gilligan's Island.*"

"Listen to scientists, not rich people."

I laughed, threw up my hands in defeat, and signaled to the waiter for another round.

"Our scientists have done things which nobody's ever done before."

—Jurassic Park

"That *Gilligan's Island* answer got me thinking," said the Vulcan. "Why is it that people are so much more comfortable following the lead of corporations or the rich rather than scientists?"

"Scientists aren't as glamorous," I said.

"And they don't have good PR," said the Wookiee. "Unless you count Big Pharma buying airtime during the nightly news and game shows for commercials about erectile dysfunction, psoriasis, or antidepressants."

"Personally, I'd pay more attention to Big Pharma if they had Big Barda as a spokeswoman," said the Hobbit gleefully.

The Vulcan stared at the Hobbit. "Riiiiight. But for now, I spend more time googling my symptoms after watching network TV because of those commercials! Anyway, look at practically every disaster movie: from *2012* to *The Day After Tomorrow*, it's the scientists who are, at best, humored or, at worst, ignored. Spock was a science officer and his captain and crew trusted him. But when Doctor Zarkov warned NASA that the natural disasters were being caused by something off-planet, they fired him!"

"That didn't really give him the right to kidnap Flash Gordon and Dale and take them to outer space," I said.

"Agreed. That . . . that was a bad thing he did. But he knew he was right!" I raised my own eyebrow at the Vulcan.

"About the science, not the kidnapping. But we already talked about villains thinking they're heroes. Let's look at Jeff Goldblum now," the Vulcan said.

"I could! All day long!" exclaimed the Wookiee. Our shared love for Jeff Goldblum was honest and true. We toasted to his continued success. "To Goldblum!"

"Nobody listened to him in *Jurassic Park* and nobody listened to him in *Independence Day*. And look what happened!

"Then, of course, there's Jor-El," the Vulcan continued. "He was a scientist. His whole *thing* was science. But nobody wanted to hear from the scientist who kept telling them that science was showing that Krypton was doomed. And what happened?" he asked.

"Krypton was doomed!" I answered.

"Doomed!" the Vulcan agreed. "And don't forget Vought International from *The Boys*. They intentionally fed children Compound V to give them powers. Or even the rebooted *Planet of the Apes* movies. If they'd listened to the scientists, the Simian Flu could have been contained! We've already established that corporations are only in it for themselves, and it's clear that actual real-life governments can be taken over by dictators and lunatics, but science is science. It's based on facts." The Vulcan sat back in his chair. "If we don't trust science, we're all doomed."

"And that," said the Hobbit, "is a hard pill to swallow. But it helps if you wash it down with another beer!"

"I'm asking you to take a leap of faith."

—Inception

"You know," I said, "Mary Poppins taught us that a spoonful of sugar helps the medicine go down."

"Better than beer?" asked the Hobbit.

"Yes. Safer, too," I replied. "I think we've all seen that to be the case when a movie or show is trying to tell us something important. Instead of just ramming the message down our throats, they package it in a fun or entertaining way." I looked at the Vulcan. "Some of *Star Trek*'s best episodes were the ones that tackled social issues real people face every day, from racism to war to gender identity to processing feelings and emotions. But they were told through a lens that made the stories accessible and palatable, so they didn't come off as preachy or political."

"Except for that space Nazi episode," said the Hobbit.

"Well, there's always an exception that proves the rule! *Star Wars* is just as effective at imparting lessons: it makes lots of statements about democracy and trade and spirituality," I said.

"There was a scene in *Attack of the Clones* where Padmé and Anakin are talking about how politicians should work for the people. Anakin suggests that if they can't agree, they should be made to, which Padmé reminds him is a dictatorship," said the Vulcan.

"Exactly," I agreed. "And *Battlestar Galactica* is constantly wrestling with politics, the will of the people, and the separations between church and state. *The Matrix* shows us that when no amount of sugar will help the blue pill or the red pill go down, you've got to suck it up and swallow it on your own. It's asking people to make the choice to either look for the truth—in government, in technology, in your relationships and everyday lives—or continue to just accept that what you're being told is the truth."

"But wouldn't you agree," asked the Elder, "that some things simply cannot be explained? That there are some things that require a little bit of faith?"

"How's that?" asked the Hobbit.

The Elder thought for a moment. "Well, the Force, for one thing. The Sith and Jedi religions were adept at wielding its power, but was it ever truly explained?" The Wookiee opened their mouth. "And don't say midi-chlorians," said the Elder, anticipating the Wookiee's response, "because even if they did allow their hosts to *use* the Force, that didn't really explain where the Force *came* from.

"We were just talking about *Battlestar Galactica*," the Elder continued, "which is another example of explaining—or not explaining—the inexplicable. The entire reboot was based on a complex belief system of ancient gods and goddesses, and a faith that they would be led to a new, safe, and promised place to live called Earth. Faith and science worked together on the show to get the survivors, and the Cylons, to the end of their story so they could start anew on a new planet. Magic and unexplained forces are all throughout Middle-earth," the Elder went on, "especially in all of the fabled rings. Magic may be science that isn't understood yet, but, well, come on.

"There are tons of unexplained powers and entities in everything we watch, read, and play," said the Elder. "But I guess the best example of what I'm talking about can be found in any of the *Indiana Jones* movies. Indy was a man of letters. But each of his big-screen adventures challenged him to look beyond his understanding of science to accept that there were higher powers at work. Whether it was the Ark of the Covenant, Sankara Stones, or the Holy Grail, Indy was repeatedly forced to adapt his worldview to include things that were beyond his understanding."

"But what about the alien skull? That's science," said the Hobbit.

"Science, yes, but from so long ago that it was seen as nothing less than a higher power, just like the Asgardians who came to Earth centuries ago. They weren't actual gods, but they were treated as such. Wonder Woman's mythos is reliant on ancient gods and goddesses, and as we said earlier, Sybok's belief in a higher power led him to do things most Vulcans wouldn't think of. And even if they don't believe in God, a divine spirit, or organized religion, lots of people believe in a higher power. Whether it's a cause, or fate, karma, patriotism, guardian angels, the spirits of loved ones who have passed on, or even a Dungeon Master, people look to higher powers to get them through tough times and help them celebrate good times.

"Pop culture encourages us to believe in *something*," said the Elder. "And that belief, that faith in something bigger, can take many forms. Truth. Science. Honesty. Faith. All of the pop culture touchstones we've been discussing are wonderful means to escape and take a break from our everyday lives, but they can also give us hope, faith, and wrap some challenging issues within their spandex and capes."

"What we do in life . . . echoes in eternity."

—Gladiator

The waiter returned with more food and drinks, pausing for a long moment as he placed a cocktail glass in front of the Wookiee.

"Are you OK?" they asked him. "Do you need to sit down?"

He shook it off. "No, no, sorry. I don't know what happened. I just got the weirdest sense of déjà vu. That ever happen to you? I could have sworn I heard you say 'spandex and capes' just like that earlier."

The Elder waved his hand toward the empty room. "You've been working here in the middle of a con, all day—I'd be surprised if you hadn't heard 'spandex and capes' a thousand times already."

"I guess?" he mused, walking away.

We looked around. The tavern looked almost exactly as it had when I first arrived. But now that I thought of it, I couldn't quite tell how long I'd been there. Hours? Minutes? How much had we drunk?

Eaten? It felt like we were living in a bubble somehow outside of time and space. I started to feel the waiter's sense of déjà vu myself. "I'm sort of feeling it, too," I said.

"That's just life," said the Wookiee. "I mean, think about it: if one original movie or show or book comes out, without fail, a million more that are just like it will come out right after. One hit book about a vampire romance and then BLAM!, five more series and movies, all about vampire romances. Zombies in Elizabethan England? Here they are in a comedy! Space opera? Here's five more. And then there are the spin-offs and reboots and reimaginings: A new *Spider-Man* trilogy. A newer, gritty *Batman*. *Stargate*, but in a different location. *Altered Carbon*, but with a different lead character. A movie sequel may have one crossover character to tie it into the original, like plopping Jimmy Olsen into *Supergirl*, but maybe it's just the title that connects it, like *American Psycho 2*. Some good, some bad, but most cut from the same astro-cloth, and all variations on a theme. Don't get me wrong, though: I love most of it. Especially the totally original ones like *Babylon 5* or *The Expanse* or *Farscape*. But, out of them all, *Battlestar Galactica* is the best example of what I'm talking about—something new that echoes something familiar."

The Wookiee took a sip of their drink. "The original was great. Great battles, interesting stories, super character names, all that. And the reboot was just as great, if not greater. Greater battles, *really* interesting stories, super characters—named the same things as in the first version, but making sense within the context of the show's greater mythology. They were sort of faint echoes of the first series. Plus, in the new series, the Cylons had evolved from giant hulking metal things to things that looked like people—people who could never really die because, if their bodies were destroyed, their consciousnesses would be uploaded into other bodies. Bodies that looked just like their other bodies. They, too, would become a sort of echo of themselves.

"Many people say history repeats itself, but I think it echoes," continued the Wookiee. "There were lots of beats in J.J. Abrams's *Star Trek* and *Star Wars* films that were similar to the originals, and having returning characters made *The Hobbit* and *Lord of the Rings* trilogies feel like one six-film epic. No two things are exactly alike and no two scenarios are precisely the same, but they can be similar enough for similar-enough story lines to play out, points to be made, and goals to be reached. I think the same thing happens in our individual lives with people. As we said earlier, we meet hundreds or thousands of people in our lives, but the ones who matter the most to us are the ones we feel a connection with, and it just makes sense that we generally connect with the same kinds of people. I don't mean like when we're dating and have a specific 'type'; I mean overall personalities. Look at us—we're all nerds."

"Hey!" said the Hobbit. "I prefer Homo Superior."

"And I respect that," said the Wookiee. "But because we're all like-minded, we seek out and find other like-minded people. You're of course surrounded by different kinds of people all day, but I bet you and most of your circles usually have similar views on lots of things, especially the things that matter. There's always room for disagreement and healthy discussion and productive conversations, but if your points of view or core beliefs differ too much, there isn't going to be enough common ground to build a relationship on. So the people closest to you, the ones you keep encountering over and over again, the ones you attract and who attract you, are all variations on a theme. Echoes of the same person. Different generations of the same twelve Cylon models."

"And that's one case where they really *shouldn't* have listened to the scientist," said the Vulcan.

"Well," said the Wookiee, cocking their head and smiling. At least I think they were smiling. "Nobody's perfect!"

Go, Speed Round, Go Go Go Go!

I t was time for another speed round. "This one," I said to the Elder, "is Disney."

"Ooooooooh," said the Vulcan, Wookiee, and Hobbit. The Elder just stared into my eyes.

"Ooooooooh," they all said again, as a chorus.

I scanned the room for an idea to start me off and spotted "fish tacos" on the menu.

"*Finding Nemo.*"

"When things are tough, just keep swimming through them to the other side."

"*The Little Mermaid.*"

"You can't dictate your children's lives for them."

"*Frozen.*"

"Live out loud."

"*The Hunchback of Notre Dame.*"

"Practice what you preach. Also, just because you're alone doesn't mean you have to be lonely."

"*Pocahontas.*"

"History is written by the victors."

"*101 Dalmatians.*"

"Pets are family."

"*Lilo & Stitch*, and don't say 'family means nobody gets left behind.'"

"Imperfect pets are perfect pets."

"OK, that was good. *Cinderella.*"

"Always wear the right shoes."

"*Sleeping Beauty.*"

"You have no right to tell someone how they feel."

"*Coco.*"

"Memories are blessings."

"*Toy Story.*"

"Nostalgia is more than just a fleeting pleasant remembrance; it's a powerful connection to happiness."

"*The Lion King.*"

"Families . . . am I right?"

"*Alice in Wonderland.*"

"Take medications only as prescribed. Do not take if you're allergic. Side effects may include diminished size, delusions, and decapitation."

"*Peter Pan.*"

"You have to grow old but you don't have to grow up."

"I give up! You win!" I exclaimed.

The Elder beamed. "It's a wonder what having an annual pass and a streaming service can do," he said.

"Worth it!"

—Deadpool

"**A**re you this good at everything?" I asked.

"Not everything," the Elder said, signaling for the waiter. "Another round!" the Elder said as he approached. He pointed to me. "And this one's on him."

"Nobody's good at *everything*," said the Hobbit.

The Vulcan made space on the table for the new glasses. "But some people are good at lots of things. And everyone's good at *something*. Remember what we were saying earlier about *Jaws*? Each character brought his own skill set to the situation. I've always loved the way secondary characters in pop culture contribute to stories. Not sidekicks, but just regular, ordinary people who are somehow tapped to do something they do really well. Some people are super-smart hackers like the Lone Gunmen, others are really good cops like Commissioner Gordon, and some are amazing detectives like Sherlock Holmes or reporters like Lois Lane.

"But there are other characters," the Vulcan continued, "like Ma and Pa Kent, or Alfred, or Aunt May or Amanda Grayson, or Laura Barton or Joyce Summers, who have the ability to ground the hero, keeping them tethered to their humanity, their morality, their sense of purpose and self, and centered on who they are. But, regardless of what they can or can't do, all of these characters are important to the story. Everyone aboard *Voyager*, the *Enterprise*, or even the *Defiant* had an integral part to play in Starfleet. Everyone who could swing an ax or use a bow and arrow was valuable when fighting the orcs at Helm's Deep. Each civilian or member of the Rebellion played an important role in the fights over Scarif, Endor, and Exegol. And what's more, each of those people knew how valuable they were. I think we need to treat everyone like a collectible that can offer all of us, and the greater good, something valuable, and that they deserve our respect."

The Hobbit smiled. "I guess if the Witch King had appreciated Éowyn's value and understood that she could be an actual threat to him, things would have played out differently."

The Vulcan agreed. "But Éowyn had always—*always*—known her value, and seen the value in others. Whether it was leading the women and children to safety, supporting Aragorn, or nursing Théoden back to health and then, later, intentionally defying him and joining the battle. She even *saw* Merry when nobody else did! She understood that everyone who wanted to fight should be allowed to fight. She understood and appreciated and supported the value of everyone."

"And don't forget about Peggy Carter," said the Wookiee. "After World War II, she was always battling against misogyny—so much so that she said, and I'm paraphrasing here, that whether or not anyone else would acknowledge it, she knew her own value."

"But right now," said the Hobbit, "I'm glad there's value in other people's money because I'm a little short."

I laughed. "I mean," he clarified, "that I'm a little light on funds right now."

"I'll add it to your tab," said the Wookiee.

"It's funny that money has value, though, isn't it?" I asked.

The Elder thought for a moment. "It's true. Things only have value because people decide they do. Think about how many people won't open a box because they think whatever is inside is going to lose its value. Value to who? They're willing to spend hundreds of dollars on something that they'll never actually see or touch because breaking the seal or somehow unwrapping it is going to make it worth less money than they paid for it. I guess that could be true if the only value you place on it is what other people think it's worth, but have you ever seen the joy of a kid playing with an action figure?"

"Some grown-ups, too!" I said.

"Yes!" agreed the Elder. "I cannot wait to rip open a box and look at and feel what I got. I love posing and positioning things on my shelves at home so I can enjoy them. But some people—let's face it, a lot of people—just cannot understand that. They'd rather keep whatever they have pristine and free of fingerprints on the off chance that, someday, they'll resell it or pass it down to their kids. The collectors are just that: collectors. And just like the Collector who lives in Knowhere, they're not *enjoyers*. They're not allowing themselves to fully experience or get to know what's in their collection. The true value of a thing is not how much money you paid for it, or how much money you can get for it, but what it means to you."

The Elder held up his hand and pointed to his ring. "This was my grandfather's. I never remember seeing him without it. And when he died, my grandmother gave it to me. I had it appraised a few years ago, and it turns out it's worth a few hundred dollars, tops. But to me, it's priceless. Sauron's rings were imbued with dark magic. Magic so powerful it enchanted and destroyed elves, dwarves, and men.

But to a Hobbit? It was magic, for sure, but not necessarily evil. All encompassing, mysterious, and possibly dangerous, sure, but Bilbo never realized, and I mean that in both senses of the word, the ring's true power because he was constitutionally incapable of such malevolence. Princess Leia had to remind her fellow Rebels that they shouldn't underestimate droids. Because she understood that they were more than just mindless 'things'; they were valuable. And certainly worth more than Lars ever paid with his hard-earned money!"

"I like the idea of no money," said the Hobbit. "I mean, I should just be given things, right? I'm a nice guy."

"Very nice," said the Vulcan. "And very lazy."

"I resemble that remark!" said the Hobbit, toasting his friend.

"There's something to be said for hard work and the satisfaction of a job well done," said the Elder.

"I agree," said the Vulcan. "I mean, everyone talks about how easy it would have been for Gandalf to have just called on the giant eagles to take the Fellowship of the Ring straight to Mordor. It would have saved months of walking. But if they did that, if they took the easy way out, then would it all have mattered as much?" The Vulcan looked around the table for an answer. I could tell the Hobbit thought it would have, so I spoke up.

"I mean, there's hardly any money used in *Star Trek* because, at least for the members of the United Federation of Planets, there's so little want. Food, shelter, clothing—it's all available for no cost. Replicators have made things a lot easier, so people can work and devote their lives not to money, but to the satisfaction of a job well done. To better themselves and society. To boldly go!"

"But if there is a shortcut . . . ?" asked the Hobbit.

The Vulcan sighed. "If there's a shortcut then you're missing out on everything along the way. Every chance to better yourself, too. If Glinda had told Dorothy to click her heels at the very beginning of the movie, she never would have discovered that there wasn't any place like home. She had to learn it for herself."

"And going back to what we were just talking about, about the value of things," said the Hobbit, "though Dorothy may have thought her ruby slippers were pretty, and pretty important, she never thought they were as important as they actually were because she didn't value them in the same way as any of the witches."

"So you agree with me?" asked the Vulcan. "That the journey is as important as the destination, and a job well done is as good as a paycheck?"

"Oh gosh, no," said the Hobbit. "She could have sold those things for a pile of emeralds and clicked herself back home before anyone could stop her."

The Vulcan slumped in his seat. "Just forget it."

"Mark and remember."

—*Clash of the Titans*

"I've been thinking a lot about forgetting recently," said the Wookiee.

"You just remembered that now?" asked the Hobbit.

The Wookiee smiled, or at least I think they did. "I did! As I was getting ready for my trip out here, I was trying to remember, without looking at the schedule, all of the panels I was going to try to attend. Not for any other reason than to test myself and pass the time, really. And as I did that, I tried to remember all of the other panels I'd attended over the years. Some of them were easy to remember—the big ones about the new Marvel slate or the Superman and Batman matchup we'd all wanted, or even the new *Star Trek* series—but other than those, I had a really tough time remembering what I'd seen. They all seemed so important at the time. A lot like the show or movie or game that was hot at the moment. But now that I think about it, within the framework of everything we've been talking about tonight, I think I understand something now.

"There's a lot to enjoy in pop culture," continued the Wookiee. "All the movies, shows, books, whatever. But not all of it can go on forever; there's a life span to everything. So it's the ones that you feel a real connection with, the ones that speak to you or show you something unique, or even provide comfort, that mean the most to you. And, I guess, that's kind of like people, right? We meet thousands of people in our lives and have relationships with a lot of them."

"This isn't the place for slut shaming!" said the Hobbit.

"You know what I mean," said the Wookiee. "Relationships like the ones with people you see every year at a convention or, like we were just talking about, work buddies, or the barista from your favorite coffee shop, or the other commuters you see on the train every morning. Yeah, romantic relationships are important, sure, but for the most part, people exit your life as quickly as they enter it. It's the ones who matter that stick around, and the ones whose absences you feel the most profoundly.

"I've seen hundreds of sci-fi movies," the Wookiee went on, "but at the end of the day, I really only *love* a few of them. There are literally thousands of superheroes out there, but I really only want to talk about some of them. Some shows last for six seasons and a movie and are still talked about. Some franchises are over fifty years old and still relevant. But some shows can last multiple seasons and, whether because they lost steam or just had a bad final episode, are just . . . gone. Forgotten. Sometimes even a joke. And isn't that like some friendships? They can start off great, but sometimes you just go your separate ways or there's a fight that ends things. I don't remember every elementary school classmate I had, but I still check out the Twitter feeds of the ones that I shared something special with. And I think the shows that give us, years or decades later, a reunion episode or special online thing, or even a new series, can go one of two ways: either it's seen as the return of a good friend, or it's met with a shrug, as if a guy you met at a concert sends you a friend request.

"As much as you can have relationships with the people that come in and out of your life, you can have relationships with a movie or a book or a game. It can be just as real, just as important, and just as forgettable."

"I, for one, have no memory of this place," said the Elder with a wry smile, "but I will surely remember you, my friend."

The Wookiee put their hand on the Elder's and smiled. At least I think they smiled.

Go, Speed Round, Go Go Go Go Go!

"We've been here long enough," said the Elder, "that I think you get it. You can see how much we've learned from pop culture. Are you ready for a speed round of your own?"

I looked to the Vulcan, the Wookiee, and the Hobbit for help, but they just smiled—or at least I think the Wookiee smiled, I couldn't quite tell—and nodded. "OK, I'll try."

"There is no try," said the Wookiee, "only do."

"Ready?" asked the Elder.

"Hit me," I said.

"*Harry Potter.*"

"We learn more in school than what's in textbooks."

"*Blade Runner.*"

"Looks can be deceiving."

"*Excalibur.*"

"Don't sleep with your boss's wife."

"*Watchmen.*"

"Absolute power corrupts absolutely. Also, systemic racism is a thing that must be confronted, and the American educational system is woefully deficient in teaching us about American—and especially African American—history."

"There's a lot to unpack in all of that, but yes! *Avatar*."

"Which one?"

"Cameron."

"Don't pollute."

"*Avatar*."

"Which one?"

"The other one."

"Whitewashing and cultural appropriation rob society of richness and texture, but also strong women are cool."

"Again, a lot to unpack, but right on all counts. *Steven Universe*."

"Gender is a construct."

"Mr. Rogers."

"Be kind."

"Bob Ross."

"Be creative."

"LeVar Burton."

"Reading can take you anywhere."

"You."

"What?"

"You," the Elder repeated. "What can we learn from you?"

"Here at the end of all things."

—The Lord of the Rings: The Return of the King

I sat there in stunned silence, contemplating what I'd been asked. Somehow, at some point, the waiter had come and gone. Our table was empty. In fact, all of the tables were empty and most of the lights were turned off. The waiter was doing his final wipe-down of the bar, thanking us for the large tip we left on the bill that had somehow, sometime, been paid, and the night was over. There was only thing left to do, and I didn't know how to do it.

I'd started the evening alone. And somehow, for some period of time that I couldn't quantify, I'd been transported to a place, a mindset where I found new ways to look at the movies and shows I thought I already knew everything about. I looked at the Vulcan, the Wookiee, the Hobbit, and the Elder and no longer saw them as cosplayers taking pity on a weary traveler, but as fellow travelers and friends. I wondered what I would find the next time I opened up the book I traveled with. Would my old friend show me something new? Though I'd read it hundreds of times, had I ever really understood it?

I had no answer for the Elder. None that I felt I could articulate, anyway. The others had done it so well: Live like a Vulcan. Love like a Wookiee. Laugh like a Hobbit. Guide like an Elder. But me?

"I think," I said as we all gathered our things and walked toward the door, "I think before tonight I'd have said I was just me. Movie-, book-, TV-loving me. But after tonight, after unboxing all of the stories, the characters, and the experiences I carry around with me, that's changed. I know, now, at the end of all things, that I am what I've learned to be. And I've learned to hope like a Rebel. To explore like an Officer. To see like an Elf."

They smiled. I could tell the Wookiee was smiling this time, too.

"Go on," said the Elder.

"To protect and defend like an Avenger. To learn like a first year at Hogwarts. To be as determined as the Spaniard in Florin. To be as filled with wonder as Alice, as—"

"OK," interrupted the Hobbit, "that's enough. This never-ending story has to end sometime."

I agreed, and we said our goodnights as I opened the door for them.

"Who taught you that?" asked the Elder, gesturing toward the door with a wink.

I heard the faint sounds of John Williams's *Harry Potter* score and watched them walk through the hotel lobby and lost track of them the moment they stepped out onto the crowded street. There were still hundreds of convention-goers out there, and I wondered how many of them had had a night like mine.

I waited for the elevator with a group made of two zombies, a witch, and a steampunker, and chatted with them about their day, their favorite panels, and how they were preparing to camp outside the convention center to be first in line for the next morning's panels. The doors opened to my floor and I wished them all luck on their overnight. Once safely inside my dark and quiet room, I left my clothes in a pile next to my backpack and got into the shower. As the hot water washed the day away, I realized that the tsunami of anxiety that I'd braced for when first meeting the Elder, Vulcan, Wookiee, and Hobbit had never come. It just sort of . . . disappeared without me ever thinking about it.

I toweled off, put on my T-shirt and shorts, and set my phone's alarm to go off at 8 AM, giving me plenty of time to eat something and get to the convention center by nine without having to rush—too much, at least. I grabbed my old book friend from my backpack, slid into bed, and propped pillows up behind my head, settling in to read until I drifted off to sleep. But this night, after a few sentences, I saw something I'd never seen before.

Acknowledgments

Thank you to my very own superteam: Brigid Pearson, Heather Butterfield, Vy Tran, Glenn Yeffeth, Jennifer Canzoneri, Adrienne Lang, Leah Wilson, and Jay Kilburn. My RP^2 teammate, Rachel "The Phantastic" Phares was always there to save me. Michael Fedison was a fierce Defender of the Oxford Comma. Aaron Edmiston rescued each orphan and widow. Master of the Arts Jason Kayser conjured a crossover cover worthy of the gods.

Thank you to my family, superfriends, and colleagues for understanding that I needed to see a movie on opening night, watch a show's final episode as it was airing, and have the right action figure on my shelf. They are my origin story, and I try to make them proud by using my powers for good.

Thanks to my brave and bold David for our thrilling adventures. And for always waiting for the credits to end before asking questions.

About the Author

R obb Pearlman is a pop culturalist and a #1 *New York Times* bestselling author of more than forty books for grown-ups and kids including *Life Lessons from Bob Ross, What Would Skeletor Do?, The Wit and Wisdom of Star Trek, The Rick and Morty Book of Gadgets and Inventions, I Adulted: Stickers for Grown-Ups, Movie Night Trivia, The Office: A Day at Dunder Mifflin Elementary, Bob Ross and Peapod the Squirrel,* and *Fun with Kirk and Spock.*

As a publishing professional, Robb has acquired and edited a host of pop culture and entertainment properties including *Bob Ross, Bob's Burgers, The Joker,* and *The Princess Bride.* He has edited monographs of the work and lives of award-winning animators Bill Plympton and Ralph Bakshi, and been the brand manager for *Raggedy Ann and Andy, Nancy Drew,* and *The Hardy Boys.*

Robb has had successful events and signings at pop culture conventions, bookstores, and comic book retailers across the country. He is a "crew member" on the annual Star Trek: The Cruise, was featured in National Geographic Channel's "Generation X" series, contributed to startrek.com and HuffingtonPost.com, performed at the Nerdnite Nerdtacular, and has been a guest on several pop culture blogs, podcasts, and radio shows. He serves on the Advisory Board of the MS in Publishing Program at Pace University and has served on the Board of Directors of Teachers & Writers Collaborative. You can visit Robb at robbpearlman.com.

Illustrator Credits

An Unexpected Pleasure: *Beer* by Juraj Sedlák from the Noun Project

No Choice, Huh?: *two stars* by Fatahillah from the Noun Project

You're Going to Need a Bigger Boat: *Shark Fin* by Linseed Studio from the Noun Project

You Meddling Kids: *Bicycle* by Andrejs Kirma from the Noun Project

Live Like a Vulcan: *Vulcan Salute* by HeadsOfBirds from the Noun Project

Love Like a Wookiee: *X-wing* by icon 54 from the Noun Project

Laugh Like a Hobbit: *Hobbit* by HeadsOfBirds from the Noun Project

How We Face Death Is at Least as Important as How We Face Life: *growth* by JunGSa from the Noun Project

I Found the Seer's Body in the Quicksand: *drown* by Berkah Icon from the Noun Project

Fly Casual: *Space* by Nhor from the Noun Project

Go, Speed Round, Go!: *speed* by Chintuza from the Noun Project

There Is a Clause in the Contract: *contract* by Gregor Cresnar from the Noun Project

Hire the Clown: *name* by Adrien Coquet from the Noun Project

Go, Speed Round, Go Go!: *speed* by Chintuza from the Noun Project

There Is No Good and Evil: *frankenstein* by Oksana Latysheva from the Noun Project

Punishment Means Nothing to Them: *Prison* by Andrejs Kirma from the Noun Project

Backstory Stuff: *History* by iconpixel from the Noun Project

Assemble!: *team* by Izwar Muis from the Noun Project

Go, Speed Round, Go Go Go!: *speed* by Chintuza from the Noun Project

Our Scientists Have Done Things Which Nobody's Ever Done Before: *Science* by BomSymbols from the Noun Project

I'm Asking You to Take a Leap of Faith: *yin yang* by Hea Poh Lin from the Noun Project

What We Do in Life . . . Echoes in Eternity: *eternity* by tezar tantular from the Noun Project

Go, Speed Round, Go Go Go Go!: *speed* by Chintuza from the Noun Project

Worth It!: *Value* by Nawicon from the Noun Project

Mark and Remember: *reminder* by Ryan Sun from the Noun Project

Go, Speed Round, Go Go Go Go Go!: *speed* by Chintuza from the Noun Project

Here at the End of All Things: *end* by Adrien Coquet from the Noun Project

A Vulcan, a Wookiee,

and a Hobbit will return